A Celebration of
Christmas

**FLAME TREE
PUBLISHING**

Contents

Introduction 4

'O Come All Ye Faithful' 6

Festive Facts 8

'Winter Wonderland' 9

A Christmas Prayer 11

Christmas Craft 11

'Away In A Manger' 12

A Christmas Prayer 13

Christmas Recipe: Egg Nog 14

Christmas Is Coming 15

Festive Fact 15

'Silent Night' 16

The Shepherds Had An Angel 18

Festive Fact 19

Christmas Recipe: Mince Pies 20

Joy To The World 22

A Christmas Prayer 23

Ceremonies For Christmas 24

Nativity 25

Recipe: Christmas Pudding 26

Christmas Craft 28

'God Rest Ye Merry Gentlemen' 29

'The Twelve Days Of Christmas' 30

Festive Facts 32

A Christmas Carol 33

A Christmas Prayer 35

'We Wish You A Merry Christmas' 35

'Hark The Herald Angels Sing!' 36

A Christmas Prayer 39

Christmas Tip 39

'Jingle Bells' 42

Christmas Bells 44

More Christmas Customs 45

The Night Before Christmas 46

Introduction

hristmas is a very special time of year. Some of us love it; some of us find it a little more trying... Those who tire of Christmas have been worn down by its relentless commercialization; they feel a mounting pressure, year after year, to spend more and more money; they are sick and tired of the season's pop tunes piped into their ears on a loop.

However, those of us who love Christmas have managed to hold on to the childlike wonder and excitement that cannot fail to stir in even the most hardened of souls when faced with a crisp and still December night, snow flakes glistening on the ground, the scent of cinnamon on the air and carols ringing out from rosy-cheeked singers. The spirit of love and generosity that still pervades when we brush aside the cynicisms is something to be held dear.

This part of the year has long been a time for celebration. Whether you use it to remember the birth of Christ or simply rejoice in the festivities that brighten up a dark winter, there is much to enjoy. We all have our favourite

things about Christmas, from the magical tree blinking and twinkling its myriad colours and the glee of children as they open the presents underneath, to the evocative poems and songs – not to mention the tasty food, rich with spices and flavours that are quintessential Christmas.

This delightful book celebrates the holiday season with a treasure trove of nostalgia, including recipes, carols, poems, prayers, classic jokes, crafts and fascinating customs from around the around the world. **Indulge!**

'O Come All Ye Faithful'

O Come All Ye Faithful
Joyful and triumphant,
O come ye, O come ye to Bethlehem.
Come and behold Him,
Born the King of Angels;
O come, let us adore Him,
O come, let us adore Him,
O come, let us adore Him,
Christ the Lord.

O Sing, choirs of angels,
Sing in exultation,
Sing all that hear in heaven God's holy word.
Give to our Father glory in the Highest;
O come, let us adore Him,
O come, let us adore Him,
O come, let us adore Him,
Christ the Lord.

All Hail! Lord, we greet Thee,
Born this happy morning,
O Jesus! for evermore be Thy name adored.
Word of the Father, now in flesh appearing;
O come, let us adore Him,
O come, let us adore Him,
O come, let us adore Him,
Christ the Lord.

Lyrics by John Francis Wade (1711–86)
Music by John Reading (c. 1685–1764)

Hullo! Father Christmas
Are you there?

Festive Facts

Why do some people eat turkey at Christmas?

Once, roast goose or boar head would have been the central dish on any British Christmas menu, but this changed in 1526 when a trader named William Strickland imported six turkeys from the US. He sold them for tuppence each and they became popular because they were tasty and practical. They were a good alternative to beef and chicken because cows were of more use alive and chickens were costly.

Why does Father Christmas wear red?

In 1863, the cartoonist Thomas Nast began a series of drawings in *Harper's Weekly*, based on 'The Night Before Christmas', in which Santa Claus, as he had now become known, could be seen with flowing beard and fur garments. Around 1869, he turned up for the first time in a bright red suit, with a white belt, but he was not invariably dressed in red until the Coca Cola corporation appropriated him for an advertising campaign that began in 1931, and ran every Christmas for 35 years. That is also when the reindeer became full size.

Christmas Cracker

What happens if you eat too many Christmas decorations?
You get Tinsel-itis!

'Winter Wonderland' (extract)

Sleigh bells ring, are you listening,
In the lane, snow is glistening
A beautiful sight,
We're happy tonight.
Walking in a winter wonderland.

Gone away is the bluebird,
Here to stay is a new bird
He sings a love song,
As we go along,
Walking in a winter wonderland.

In the meadow we can build a snowman,
Then pretend that he is Parson Brown

In the meadow we can build a snowman,
And pretend that he's a circus clown
We'll have lots of fun with mister snowman,
Until the other kids knock him down.

When it snows, ain't it thrilling,
Though your nose gets a chilling
We'll frolic and play, the Eskimo way,
Walking in a winter wonderland.

Music by Felix Bernard (1897–1944)

Lyrics by Richard B. Smith (1901–35)

A Christmas Prayer

oving Father, Help us remember the birth of Jesus, that we may share in the song of angels, the gladness of the shepherds, and the worship of the wise men. Close the door of hate and open the door of love all over the world. Let kindness come with every gift and good desires with every greeting.

Deliver us from evil by the blessing which Christ brings, and teach us to be merry with clean hearts. May the Christmas morning make us happy to be Thy children, and the Christmas evening bring us to our beds with grateful thoughts, forgiving and forgiven, for Jesus' sake, **Amen!**

by Robert Louis Stevenson (1850–94)

Christmas Customs

In Holland, Father Christmas does not arrive on a sleigh drawn by flying reindeer; instead he travels by boat.

Christmas Craft

How To Make Pomanders

Pomanders have been used since Medieval times for filling rooms with beautiful fragrance. To make a pomander, use a toothpick or knitting needle to make holes in an orange or other round fruit, and then push cloves into them. It's best to space the cloves evenly and use quite a few; you can always arrange them into patterns. If you'd like to add some other scents to your pomander then simply put some spices (such as cinnamon, nutmeg or orris root) into a resealable plastic bag. Next place your pomander into the bag and shake until covered in the spices, and allow to dry in a warm place. Then display however you wish.

'Away In A Manger'

Away in a manger,
No crib for His bed
The little Lord Jesus
Laid down His sweet head

The stars in the bright sky
Looked down where He lay
The little Lord Jesus
Asleep on the hay

The cattle are lowing
The poor Baby wakes
But little Lord Jesus
No crying He makes

I love Thee, Lord Jesus
Look down from the sky
And stay by my side,
'Til morning is nigh.

Be near me, Lord Jesus,
I ask Thee to stay
Close by me forever
And love me I pray

Bless all the dear children
In Thy tender care
And take us to heaven
To live with Thee there

Anon.
Music by William J. Kirkpatrick

Festive Fact

The Puritan Ban on Christmas

In 1647 Oliver Cromwell enforced an Act of
Parliament banning Christmas celebrations! The
Puritans thought that Christmas celebrations
were wasteful and would erode core Christian
beliefs. The ban was not lifted until 1660.

A Christmas Prayer

In the peace of this season our spirits are joyful: With the beasts and angels, the shepherds and stars, with Mary and Joseph we sing God's praise. By your coming may the hungry be filled with good things, and may our table and home be blessed. Bless us O Lord, and these Thy gifts, which we are about to receive from Thy bounty through Christ our Lord. **Amen**.

Anon.

Christmas Recipe: Egg Nog

Serves 1

Ingredients
1 large egg
1 tbsp caster sugar
50 ml/2 fl oz brandy or medium sherry
300 ml/½ pt milk
freshly grated nutmeg

Whisk the egg and sugar together until well blended, then slowly whisk in the brandy or sherry. Heat the milk to just below boiling point. Carefully stir into the egg mixture then pour into a heatproof dish and serve immediately sprinkled with a little freshly grated nutmeg.

Cook's tip:

To make enough for 4 servings, use 3 medium eggs with 2–3 tablespoons sugar (or to taste) with 150 ml/¼ pint spirits and 900 ml/1½ pints milk.

Christmas Is Coming

Christmas is coming,
The geese are getting fat,
Please put a penny
In the old man's hat.

If you haven't got a penny,
A ha'penny will do,
If you haven't got a ha'penny,
Then God bless you.

by Edith Nesbit Bland (1858–1924)

Festive Fact

What makes a 'White Christmas'?

According to the UK's Met Office the official definition of a White Christmas is for a single snowflake to be observed falling in the 24 hours of 25 December. This is the standard definition used by betting companies to decide whether or not to pay out for this most popular of novelty bets.

'Silent Night'

Silent night, holy night
All is calm, all is bright
Round yon Virgin Mother and Child
Holy Infant so tender and mild
Sleep in heavenly peace
Sleep in heavenly peace

Silent night, holy night!
Shepherds quake at the sight
Glories stream from heaven afar
Heavenly hosts sing Alleluia!
Christ, the Saviour is born
Christ, the Saviour is born

Silent night, holy night
Son of God, love's pure light
Radiant beams from Thy holy face
With the dawn of redeeming grace
Jesus, Lord, at Thy birth
Jesus, Lord, at Thy birth

Lyrics by Joseph Mohr (1792–1848)
Music by Franz Xavier Gruber (1787–1863)

The Shepherds Had An Angel

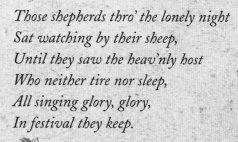

The shepherds had an angel,
The wise men had a star;
But what have I, a little child,
To guide me home from far,
Where glad stars sing together,
And singing angels are

Lord Jesus is my Guardian
so I can nothing lack;
The lambs lie in His bosom
Along life's dangerous track:
The wilful lambs that go astray
He, bleeding, brings them back.

Those shepherds thro' the lonely night
Sat watching by their sheep,
Until they saw the heav'nly host
Who neither tire nor sleep,
All singing glory, glory,
In festival they keep.

Christ watches me, His little lamb,
Cares for me day and night,
That I may be His own in heav'n,
So angels clad in white
Shall sing their Glory, glory,
For my sake in the height.

Lord, bring me nearer day by day,
Till I my voice unite,
And sing my Glory, glory,
With angels clad in white,
All Glory, glory, giv'n to Thee,
Thro' all the heav'nly height.

by Christina Rossetti (1830–94)

Christmas Cracker

What do angry mice send
to each other in December?
Cross-mouse cards!

Festive Fact

Trafalgar Square's Christmas Tree

Every year since 1947 a Christmas tree has been given to the people of London by the Norwegians in thanks for Britain's support during the Second World War.

Christmas Custom

In Latvia, Father Christmas brings presents on each of the 12 days of Christmas, beginning on Christmas Eve!

Christmas Recipe: Mince Pies

To lighten the load at Christmas, mince pies freeze well, so they can be made up to 6 weeks before. Allow to thaw thoroughly and warm for a few minutes before serving.

Makes 12

Preparation time
20 minutes, plus chilling time

Cooking time
18–20 minutes

Ingredients
225 g/8 oz plain white flour
2 tbsp caster sugar
175 g/6 oz unsalted butter, slightly softened
1 small egg, separated
225 g/8 oz prepared mincemeat
1–2 tbsp brandy, optional

Preheat the oven to 200°C/400°F/180°C fan oven/Gas Mark 6, 15 minutes before baking. Place the flour and 1 tablespoon of the sugar into a mixing bowl and make a well in the centre. Add the butter with the egg yolk and 1 tablespoon of cold water. Mix together using your hands to form a soft but not sticky dough, adding a little extra water if necessary. Turn out onto a lightly floured surface and knead until smooth. Wrap in baking paper and chill for at least 30 minutes.

When ready to cook spoon the mincemeat into a bowl and stir in 1–2 tablespoons of brandy, if using, to give a soft but not wet consistency. Roll the pastry out on a lightly floured surface. Cut into 12 7.5 cm/3 inch rounds and 12 5 cm/2 inch rounds.

Place the larger rounds in a bun tin, then spoon 1–2 teaspoons mincemeat into each. Lightly brush the edges with water and top with the smaller pastry rounds. Carefully pinch the edges together. Beat the egg white and use to brush the tops. Sprinkle with the remaining caster sugar. Make a small hole in each to allow the steam to escape.

Bake in the preheated oven for 18–20 minutes or until the pastry is golden brown. Remove from the oven and leave to cool for a few minutes, then carefully remove from the bun tin. Store in an airtight container when cold

Cook's tip:

If liked, the pastry can be made in a food processor: simply place all the ingredients in the bowl of the processor and whiz for 1–2 minutes.

Joy To The World

Joy to the world, the Lord is come!
Let earth receive her King;
Let every heart prepare Him room,
And Heaven and nature sing,
And Heaven and nature sing,
And Heaven, and Heaven, and nature sing.

Joy to the world, the Saviour reigns!
Let men their songs employ;
While fields and floods, rocks, hills and plains
Repeat the sounding joy,
Repeat the sounding joy,
Repeat, repeat, the sounding joy.

No more let sins and sorrows grow,
Nor thorns infest the ground;
He comes to make His blessings flow
Far as the curse is found,
Far as the curse is found,
Far as, far as, the curse is found.

He rules the world with truth and grace,
And makes the nations prove
The glories of His righteousness,
And wonders of His love,
And wonders of His love,
And wonders, wonders, of His love.

by Isaac Watts (1674–1748)

A Christmas Prayer

 ather God, when your precious Son became a tiny baby in a stable in Bethlehem in poverty and simplicity, you changed our world. As we imagine those surroundings, we join with the shepherds and the wise men in wonder and praise. We thank you for our material lives, praise you for our spiritual lives, and trust in you for our eternal life. **Amen.**

Anon.

Christmas Cracker

What do you get if you cross Father Christmas with a duck? A Christmas Quacker!

Ceremonies For Christmas

Come, bring with a noise,
My merry, merry boys,
The Christmas Log to the firing;
While my good Dame, she
Bids ye all be free;
And drink to your heart's desiring.

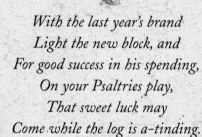

With the last year's brand
Light the new block, and
For good success in his spending,
On your Psaltries play,
That sweet luck may
Come while the log is a-tinding.

Drink now the strong beer,
Cut the white loaf here,
The while the meat is a-shredding;
For the rare mince-pie
And the plums stand by
To fill the paste that's a-kneading.

by Robert Herrick (1591–1674)

Christmas Cracker

How many elves does it take
to change a light bulb?
Ten! One to change the light bulb and
nine to stand on each other's shoulders!

Nativity

Immensity cloistered in thy dear womb,
Now leaves His well-belov'd imprisonment,
There He hath made Himself to His intent
Weak enough, now into the world to come;
But O, for thee, for Him, hath the inn no room
Yet lay Him in this stall, and from the Orient,
Stars and wise men will travel to prevent
The effect of Herod's jealous general doom.

Seest thou, my soul, with thy faith's eyes, how He
Which fills all place, yet none holds Him, doth lie
Was not His pity towards thee wondrous high,
That would have need to be pitied by thee
Kiss Him, and with Him into Egypt go,
With His kind mother, who partakes thy woe.

by John Donne (1572–1631)

Recipe: Christmas Pudding

This Christmas pudding can be made well ahead of time. If liked, one of the puddings can either be frozen or stored in a clean, cold and dark place for up to a year.

Makes
3 puddings, each serves 6

Preparation time
15 minutes, plus overnight standing

Cooking time
6 hours, plus 3 hours

Ingredients
450 g/1 lb raisins
450 g/1 lb sultanas
450 g1 lb currants
100 g/4 oz mixed cut peel
5 tbsp brandy or rum
450 g/1 lb unsalted butter, softened,
    plus 1 tbsp for greasing
450 g/1 lb dark muscovado sugar
5 medium eggs, beaten
225 g/8 oz plain white flour
1 tsp each ground cinnamon
    and mixed spice
finely grated rind and juice of 1 orange
2 tbsp black treacle, warmed
2 tbsp golden syrup, warmed
225 g/8 oz shredded suet
    (or vegetable suet)
225 g/8 oz fresh brown breadcrumbs
extra brandy or rum, to serve
brandy butter or cream, to serve
sprig of holly to garnish

Place all the dried fruits including the mixed cut peel in a mixing bowl and pour over the brandy or rum, cover and leave to stand overnight. Cut out 3 small baking or greaseproof rounds large enough to sit in the base of 3 1.2 litre/2 pint pudding basins. Lightly butter each basin with the 1 tablespoon of butter and set aside.

Cream the butter and sugar together until light and fluffy, then gradually beat in the eggs, adding a little flour after each addition. When all the eggs have been added stir in any remaining flour together with the spices and orange rind. Stir well. Stir in the black treacle and golden syrup and mix well. Add the soaked fruits together with any liquor remaining in the bowl. Stir in the shredded suet with the breadcrumbs and sufficient orange juice to give a soft dropping consistency. Cover and leave to stand overnight.

The next day, stir well, then divide between the 3 prepared pudding basins and level the tops. Make a pleat in a double sheet of baking or greaseproof paper and use to cover each pudding. Top with either a pudding cloth or double sheet of kitchen foil with a pleat in the centre.

Place in a steamer standing over a pan of gently steaming water. Steam steadily for 6 hours, remembering to top up the water as

necessary. When cooked, remove and allow to cool before re-covering as before. Store in a cool dark place until required.

At least 3 hours before ready to serve, place over a pan of gently simmering water and steam for a further 3 hours. Remove from the steamer, cool for a few minutes then invert on to a warm serving plate. Place a sprig of holly in the top. Warm a little brandy or rum, pour over the pudding and set alight. Dim the lights and take the lit pudding to the table. Serve with brandy butter or cream if liked.

Christmas Craft

How to make a Christingle

Place a red ribbon around the middle of an orange, or you can use red tape.

Cut a small cross in the top of the orange, but make sure you have something like a tray underneath it to catch any juice. Place a square of foil (75 mm/3 inches) over the cross and then wedge a candle into the cross.

Skewer soft fruits (such as raisins, sultanas and cherries) and soft sweets on four cocktail sticks and then insert them into the orange around the base of the candle.

You may need to cut a slice from the bottom of the orange so that it has a base. Store in a cool place.

What it means:

The orange represents the world and the red ribbon the blood of Jesus. The fruits and sweets on the four cocktail sticks represent the four seasons. Finally the lit candle symbolizes Christ, the light of the world.

Christmas Cracker

What do you get when you cross a snowman with a vampire? Frostbite!

'God Rest Ye Merry Gentlemen'

God rest ye merry, gentlemen
Let nothing you dismay
Remember, Christ, our Saviour
Was born on Christmas day
To save us all from Satan's power
When we were gone astray
O tidings of comfort and joy,
Comfort and joy
O tidings of comfort and joy

In Bethlehem, in Israel,
This blessed Babe was born
And laid within a manger
Upon this blessed morn
The which His Mother Mary
Did nothing take in scorn
O tidings of comfort and joy,
Comfort and joy
O tidings of comfort and joy

From God our Heavenly Father
A blessed Angel came;
And unto certain Shepherds
Brought tidings of the same:
How that in Bethlehem was born
The Son of God by Name.
O tidings of comfort and joy,
Comfort and joy
O tidings of comfort and joy

Anon.

'The Twelve Days Of Christmas'

On the **first** day of Christmas,
my true love sent to me
A partridge in a pear tree.

On the **second** day of Christmas,
my true love sent to me
Two turtle doves,
And a partridge in a pear tree.

On the **third** day of Christmas,
my true love sent to me
Three French hens,
Two turtle doves,
And a partridge in a pear tree.

On the **fourth** day of Christmas,
my true love sent to me
Four calling birds,
Three French hens,
Two turtle doves,
And a partridge in a pear tree.

On the **fifth** day of Christmas,
my true love sent to me
Five golden rings,
Four calling birds,
Three French hens,
Two turtle doves,
And a partridge in a pear tree.

On the **sixth** day of Christmas,
my true love sent to me
Six geese a-laying,
Five golden rings,
Four calling birds,
Three French hens,
Two turtle doves,
And a partridge in a pear tree.

On the **seventh** day of Christmas,
my true love sent to me
Seven swans a-swimming,
Six geese a-laying,
Five golden rings,
Four calling birds,
Three French hens,
Two turtle doves,
And a partridge in a pear tree.

On the **eighth** day of Christmas,
my true love sent to me
Eight maids a-milking,
Seven swans a-swimming,
Six geese a-laying,
Five golden rings,
Four calling birds,
Three French hens,
Two turtle doves,
And a partridge in a pear tree.

On the **ninth** day of Christmas,
my true love sent to me
Nine ladies dancing,
Eight maids a-milking,
Seven swans a-swimming,
Six geese a-laying,
Five golden rings,
Four calling birds,
Three French hens,
Two turtle doves,
And a partridge in a pear tree.

On the **tenth** day of Christmas,
my true love sent to me
Ten lords a-leaping,
Nine ladies dancing,
Eight maids a-milking,
Seven swans a-swimming,
Six geese a-laying,
Five golden rings,
Four calling birds,
Three French hens,
Two turtle doves,
And a partridge in a pear tree.

On the **eleventh** day of Christmas,
my true love sent to me
Eleven pipers piping,
Ten lords a-leaping,
Nine ladies dancing,
Eight maids a-milking,
Seven swans a-swimming,
Six geese a-laying,
Five golden rings,
Four calling birds,
Three French hens,
Two turtle doves,
And a partridge in a pear tree.

On the **twelfth** day of Christmas,
my true love sent to me
Twelve drummers drumming,
Eleven pipers piping,
Ten lords a-leaping,
Nine ladies dancing,
Eight maids a-milking,
Seven swans a-swimming,
Six geese a-laying,
Five golden rings,
Four calling birds,
Three French hens,
Two turtle doves,
And a partridge in a pear tree!

Anon.

Festive Facts

Father Christmas has many different names across the world; here are a few of them:

BELGIUM Sinterklaas

DENMARK Julemanden

FRANCE Père Noël

GERMANY Weinachtsmann

NORWAY Julenissen

SWITZERLAND Samichlaus

UNITED STATES OF AMERICA Santa Claus

A Christmas Carol (extract)

The shepherds went their hasty way,
And found the lowly stable-shed
Where the Virgin-Mother lay:
And now they checked their eager tread,
For to the Babe, that at her bosom clung,
A Mother's song the Virgin-Mother sung.

They told her how a glorious light,
Streaming from a heavenly throng,
Around them shone, suspending night!
While sweeter than a mother's song,
Blest Angels heralded the Saviour's birth,
Glory to God on high! and Peace on Earth.

She listened to the tale divine,
And closer still the Babe she pressed:
And while she cried, the Babe is mine!
The milk rushed faster to her breast:
Joy rose within her, like a summer's morn;
Peace, Peace on Earth! the Prince of Peace
   is born.

by Samuel Taylor Coleridge (1772–1834)

A Christmas Prayer

oly Creator of Trees, bless with your abundant grace this our Christmas tree as a symbol of joy. May its evergreen branches be a sign of your never-fading promises. May its colourful lights and ornaments call us to decorate with love our home and our world. May the gifts that surround this tree be symbols of the gifts we have received from the Tree of Christ's Cross. Holy Christmas tree within our home, may Joy and Peace come and nest in your branches and in our hearts. **Amen.**

Anon.

'We Wish You A Merry Christmas'

We wish you a Merry Christmas;
We wish you a Merry Christmas;
We wish you a Merry Christmas and a Happy New Year.
Good tidings we bring to you and your kin;
Good tidings for Christmas and a Happy New Year.

Oh, bring us a figgy pudding;
Oh, bring us a figgy pudding;
Oh, bring us a figgy pudding and a cup of good cheer.

We won't go until we get some;
We won't go until we get some;
We won't go until we get some, so bring some out here.

We wish you a Merry Christmas;
We wish you a Merry Christmas;
We wish you a Merry Christmas and a Happy New Year.

Anon.

A Christmas Prayer

oly Creator of Trees, bless with your abundant grace this our Christmas tree as a symbol of joy. May its evergreen branches be a sign of your never-fading promises. May its colourful lights and ornaments call us to decorate with love our home and our world. May the gifts that surround this tree be symbols of the gifts we have received from the Tree of Christ's Cross. Holy Christmas tree within our home, may Joy and Peace come and nest in your branches and in our hearts. **Amen.**

Anon.

'We Wish You A Merry Christmas'

We wish you a Merry Christmas;
We wish you a Merry Christmas;
We wish you a Merry Christmas and a Happy New Year.
Good tidings we bring to you and your kin;
Good tidings for Christmas and a Happy New Year.

Oh, bring us a figgy pudding;
Oh, bring us a figgy pudding;
Oh, bring us a figgy pudding and a cup of good cheer.

We won't go until we get some;
We won't go until we get some;
We won't go until we get some, so bring some out here.

We wish you a Merry Christmas;
We wish you a Merry Christmas;
We wish you a Merry Christmas and a Happy New Year.

Anon.

'Hark The Herald Angels Sing!' (extract)

Hark the herald angels sing
'Glory to the newborn King!
Peace on earth and mercy mild
God and sinners reconciled'
Joyful, all ye nations rise
Join the triumph of the skies
With the angelic host proclaim:
'Christ is born in Bethlehem'
Hark! The herald angels sing
'Glory to the newborn King!'

Christ by highest heav'n adored
Christ the everlasting Lord!
Late in time behold Him come
Offspring of a Virgin's womb
Veiled in flesh the Godhead see
Hail the incarnate Deity
Pleased as man with man to dwell
Jesus, our Emmanuel
Hark! The herald angels sing
'Glory to the newborn King!'

Lyrics by Charles Wesley (1707–88)
Music by Felix Mendelssohn (1809–47)

A Christmas Prayer

 ternal God, this joyful day is radiant with the brilliance of your one true light. May that light illuminate our hearts and shine in our words and deeds. May the hope, the peace, the joy, and the love represented by the birth in Bethlehem fill our lives and become part of all that we say and do. May we share the divine life of your son Jesus Christ, even as he humbled himself to share our humanity. Bless us and the feast that You have provided for us, let us be thankful for the true gift of Christmas, your Son. **Amen.**

Anon.

Christmas Cracker

Knock Knock
Who's there?
Wenceslas
Wenceslas who?
Wenceslas train home?

Christmas Customs

Before the fall of Communism in Russia it was New Year that was celebrated (with presents from 'Father Frost') instead of Christmas.

Christmas Tip

When all the festivities are done and you're packing away your decorations and lights, make sure you don't rush the job. Take time over tricky items like Christmas tree lights, you'll be thankful you did when next Christmas comes around!

'Jingle Bells'

Dashing through the snow
In a one horse open sleigh
O'er the fields we go
Laughing all the way
Bells on bob tails ring
Making spirits bright
What fun it is to laugh and sing
A sleighing song tonight

Oh, jingle bells, jingle bells
Jingle all the way
Oh, what fun it is to ride
In a one horse open sleigh
Jingle bells, jingle bells
Jingle all the way
Oh, what fun it is to ride
In a one horse open sleigh

A day or two ago
I thought I'd take a ride
And soon Miss Fanny Bright
Was seated by my side
The horse was lean and lank
Misfortune seemed his lot
We got into a drifted bank
And then we got upsot

Oh, jingle bells, jingle bells
Jingle all the way
Oh, what fun it is to ride
In a one horse open sleigh
Jingle bells, jingle bells
Jingle all the way
Oh, what fun it is to ride
In a one horse open sleigh yeah

Jingle bells, jingle bells
Jingle all the way
Oh, what fun it is to ride
In a one horse open sleigh
Jingle bells, jingle bells
Jingle all the way
Oh, what fun it is to ride
In a one horse open sleigh

by James Pierpont (1822–93)

Christmas Cracker

Why does Father Christmas
always go down the chimney?
Because it soots him!

43

Christmas Bells (extract)

I heard the bells on Christmas Day
Their old, familiar carols play,
And wild and sweet
The words repeat
Of peace on earth, goodwill to men!

And thought how, as the day had come,
The belfries of all Christendom
Had rolled along
The unbroken song
Of peace on earth, goodwill to men!

Till, ringing, singing on its way
The world revolved from night to day,
A voice, a chime,
A chant sublime
Of peace on earth, goodwill to men!

Then from each black, accursed mouth
The cannon thundered in the South,
And with the sound
The Carols drowned
Of peace on earth, goodwill to men!

by Henry Wadsworth Longfellow (1807–82)

More Christmas Customs

Kissing under the **mistletoe** is a custom that stems from Norse mythology, when it was used as a symbol of love and friendship.

Christmas Cracker

How do we know Santa is such a good racing car driver? Because he's always in pole position!

Fir trees have been used to celebrate winter festivals for thousands of years. During the winter solstice, Pagans used branches of it to decorate their homes as a reminder of the spring to come.

Around the world different trees are used as Christmas trees. New Zealanders often decorate the pohutukawa tree, whilst in India banana or mango trees are sometimes used.

The Night Before Christmas

T *was the night before Christmas, when all through the house...*

Not a creature was stirring, not even a mouse.
The stockings were hung by the chimney with care,
In hopes that St Nicholas soon would be there.

The children were nestled all snug in their beds,
While visions of sugar-plums danced in their heads.
And mamma in her 'kerchief, and I in my cap,
Had just settled our brains for a long winter's nap.

When out on the lawn there arose such a clatter,
I sprang from the bed to see what was the matter.
Away to the window I flew like a flash,
Tore open the shutters and threw up the sash.

The moon on the breast of the new-fallen snow
Gave the lustre of mid-day to objects below.
When, what to my wondering eyes should appear,
But a miniature sleigh, and eight tiny reindeer.

With a little old driver, so lively and quick,
I knew in a moment it must be St Nick.
More rapid than eagles his coursers they came,
And he whistled, and shouted, and called them
   by name!

'Now Dasher! now, Dancer! now, Prancer and Vixen
On, Comet! On, Cupid! On, Donner and Blitzen.
To the top of the porch! To the top of the wall!
Now dash away! Dash away! Dash away all!'

As dry leaves that before the wild hurricane fly,
When they meet with an obstacle, mount to the sky
So up to the house-top the coursers they flew,
With the sleigh full of Toys, and St Nicholas too.

And then, in a twinkling, I heard on the roof
The prancing and pawing of each little hoof.
As I drew in my head, and was turning around,
Down the chimney St Nicholas came with
   a bound.

He was dressed all in fur, from his head to his foot,
And his clothes were all tarnished with ashes and soot.
A bundle of Toys he had flung on his back,
And he looked like a peddler, just opening his pack.

His eyes – how they twinkled! His dimples
   how merry!
His cheeks were like roses, his nose like a cherry!
His droll little mouth was drawn up like a bow,
And the beard of his chin was as white as the snow.

The stump of a pipe he held tight in his teeth,
And the smoke it encircled his head like a wreath.
He had a broad face and a little round belly,
That shook when he laughed, like a bowlful
   of jelly!

He was chubby and plump, a right jolly old elf,
And I laughed when I saw him, in spite of myself!
A wink of his eye and a twist of his head,
Soon gave me to know I had nothing to dread.

He spoke not a word, but went straight to his work,
And filled all the stockings, then turned with a jerk.
And laying his finger aside of his nose,
And giving a nod, up the chimney he rose!

He sprang to his sleigh, to his team gave a whistle,
And away they all flew like the down of a thistle.
But I heard him exclaim, 'ere he drove out of sight,
'Happy Christmas to all, and to all a good-night!'

by Clement Clarke Moore (1779–1863)

Publisher and Creative Director: Nick Wells
Project Editor and Picture Research: Chelsea Edwards
Editorial: Cat Emslie and Sara Robson
Layout Design: Jake

First published in 2009 by
FLAME TREE PUBLISHING
Crabtree Hall, Crabtree Lane
Fulham, London SW6 6TY
United Kingdom

www.flametreepublishing.com

09 11 13 12 10

1 3 5 7 9 10 8 6 4 2

Flame Tree is part of The Foundry Creative Media Company Limited

© 2009 Flame Tree Publishing

A CIP record for this book is available from the British Library.

ISBN 978-1-84786-689-9

Every effort has been made to contact copyright holders. We apologize in advance for any omissions and would
be pleased to insert the appropriate acknowledgement in subsequent editions of this publication.

Picture Credits

All images courtesy of Foundry Arts, except the following:
3, 27 Joseph Clark (1834–1926), *The Christmas Pudding*, © Fine Art Photographic Library
9 David Jacobsen (1821–71), *Christmas Market*, © Fine Art Photographic Library
10 Norman Prescott Davies (1862–1915), *Christmas Fare*, © Fine Art Photographic Library
12 Pieter Coecke van Aelst (*c.* 1502–50), *Adoration of the Magi and a Nativity*, © Fine Art Photographic Library
13 artist unknown, *A Bright and Happy Christmas*, © Fine Art Photographic Library/reproduced courtesy of Eaglecrown
14 Charles Green (1804–98), *Christmas Comes But Once A Year!*, © Fine Art Photographic Library
15 Gilette (fl. 19th century), *Christmas Morning*, © Fine Art Photographic Library
21 William Macduff (1824–81), *Christmas At Home; Stirring the Christmas Pudding*, 1860, © Fine Art Photographic Library
25 Henry Raymond Thompson (fl. 1892–1904), *O Holy Night from Thee I Learn to Bear*, 1897, © The Bridgeman Art Library
28 Mary Ellen Edwards (1838–*c.* 1910), *A Christmas Message*, © Fine Art Photographic Library
33 Erik Henningsen (1855–1930), *Ostergade, Copenhagen, Denmark, Christmas Time*, 1890, © Fine Art Photographic Library
37 Daphne Allan (19th century), *Holy Star*, © The Illustrated London News Picture Library, London, UK/
The Bridgeman Art Library
38 Anton Ebert (1845–96), *Roasted Chestnuts*, © Fine Art Photographic Library
44 George Goodwin Kilburne (1839–1924), *Christmas Eve*, © Fine Art Photographic Library
45 George Sheridan Knowles (1863–1931), *Christmas*, © Fine Art Photographic Library

Printed in China